D1825046

A PLACE
of
SPRINGS

• • •

Reflections on the Journey

Suzanne Witty

WESTBOW
PRESS®
A DIVISION OF THOMAS NELSON
& ZONDERVAN

THE HOLY BIBLE, NEW INTERNATIONAL VERSION®, NIV® Copyright © 1973, 1978, 1984, 2011 by Biblica, Inc.® Used by permission. All rights reserved worldwide.

"Scripture quotations are from the ESV® Bible (The Holy Bible, English Standard Version®), copyright © 2001 by Crossway, a publishing ministry of Good News Publishers. Used by permission. All rights reserved."

WestBow Press books may be ordered through booksellers or by contacting:

WestBow Press
A Division of Thomas Nelson & Zondervan
1663 Liberty Drive
Bloomington, IN 47403
www.westbowpress.com
1 (866) 928-1240

Because of the dynamic nature of the Internet, any web addresses or links contained in this book may have changed since publication and may no longer be valid. The views expressed in this work are solely those of the author and do not necessarily reflect the views of the publisher, and the publisher hereby disclaims any responsibility for them.

Any people depicted in stock imagery provided by Getty Images are models, and such images are being used for illustrative purposes only. Certain stock imagery © Getty Images.

ISBN: 978-1-9736-4491-0 (sc)
ISBN: 978-1-9736-4493-4 (hc)
ISBN: 978-1-9736-4492-7 (e)

Library of Congress Control Number: 2018913365

Print information available on the last page.

WestBow Press rev. date: 11/21/2018

"Blessed are those whose strength is in you, whose hearts are set on pilgrimage. As they pass through the Valley of Baka, they make it a place of springs; the autumn rains also cover it with pools. They go from strength to strength, till each appears before God in Zion." Psalm 84:5-7 (NIV)

To Susan and Calvin, fellow travelers on the journey, with deep gratitude for their encouragement and support.

Contents

Journey On!

I couldn't stop long at the wayside,
Nor weary, rest long at the inn,
For Someone kept urging me onward
The path that He chose I begin.

The goal I could see in the distance
My spirit kept hopeful and bright,
A Home and a joyful reunion
Awaited in Heaven's clear light.

There loved ones all gather rejoicing,
Their own journeys' toil finally past,
While watching and cheering my progress,
They know I will make it at last!

For He has secured my safe passage,
Arrival at Home will be mine,
No matter the dark clouds that gather,
They know I will make it just fine!

As faithful I follow His bidding
And to my task ply every skill,
There will come a day, not too far away,
When to Himself call me He will.

And oh the joy on that blest meeting,
As there by His side we shall stand,

Together at last, all toil's sorrow past,
Again we shall walk hand in hand!

"Therefore, since we are surrounded by so great a cloud of witnesses, let us also lay aside every weight, and sin which clings so closely, and let us run with patience the race that is set before us, looking unto Jesus, the founder and perfecter of our faith, who for the joy that was set before Him endured the cross, despising the shame, and is seated at the right hand of the throne of God." Hebrews 12:1 (ESV)

Sola Gratia

You know just what I need, dear Lord,
You've planned it all along,
Though through the years I've cried to You
With fearful, plaintiff song.

Today was written in your Book
Before my life began,
And all my steps have ordered been,
My times ARE in Your hands.

Past days, though so important then,
Have disappeared like night,
As when the sun each morning new
Dispels the dark with light.

And thus our days have marched ahead
In ordered rank and file,
Each one according to Your Plan,
We've lived here for awhile.

Your purposes, Your Holy Name,
Our focus true have been,
As daily walking in Your Light
You've guided us again.

So as we look upon that Day
When our time here is done,

We ask no more than Your great grace
A faithful race to run.

For when the Dawn at last shall break
Upon that glorious Day,
"Pilgrim, you have honored me,"
We long to hear You Say.

"The path of the righteous is like the light of dawn, which shines brighter and brighter until full day." Proverbs 4:18 (ESV)

The Robin's Lesson

The gray of Janus shut me in ...
I could not sing with joy.
Just rousing from the featherbed
Did all my strength employ.

When to the window I was drawn ...
Some ray of light to find,
Some promise of a day begun
To ease my clouded mind.

And there beheld I at a glance,
And much to my surprise,
A passing flock of robins gay,
On my porch had arrived!

Each wore his vest of rusty red,
Each cocked his shining eye,
And gazing at my tousled head
Each one seemed to reply,

"Why look so glum, my human friend,
This January morn?
Our Heavenly Father's cared for you
Each day since you were born.

And He has deigned the seasons so
Each one its purpose holds

To guide and meld and form your life,
Refining you like gold!

So on that Day when He returns
And your life's work is done,
He'll find in you the full ripe fruit
Of work which He's begun.

So now take joy to be your strength
And praise Him in all things …
Like we who sing so joyfully,
You'll find you, too, have wings!"

"Sing to the Lord with thanksgiving; make melody to our
God on the lyre!" Psalm 147:7,8 (ESV)

The Singing Wren

Before daylight the wren did sing,
In waning night a song to bring.
Heralding the day that was to be,
She reawakened hope in me!

So small, still to the branch she clung,
Where in the winter no leaf hung,
And piped her song so merrily
Before the sun's rays she could see.

Even so, dear Father, help me, too,
Lift songs of joyful praise to You
Though in the darkness I may be,
Knowing soon the Light I'll see,

And be to others passing near
A blessed reminder they can hear,
To call them, too, to stop and raise
Their voice to You in hope and praise.

"O my Strength, I will sing praises to you, for you, O God,
are my fortress, the God who shows steadfast love." Psalm 59:17 (ESV)

Seeing Eternity In An Hour

As day began the clouds grew pink,
Which caused me there to stop and think
Of our great God's eternal plan
To bring Redemption down to man.

The early hour had gray begun,
As I arose before the sun,
Plans to begin my daily ploy,
Another day thus to enjoy.

On opening the window shade
The light burst in, and with it made
My sleepy brain begin to spin
With thoughts eternal, and akin

To promises our Lord has given
Which tell us of our home in heaven
When God makes all things new one day
And this world's tears are wiped away.

So thank you, Lord, for morning light
Which greets me after darkest night,
Reminding me of what's to come ...
That morn when we shall see the Son!

"For since the creation of the world God's invisible qualities—his
eternal power and divine nature—have been clearly seen, being
understood from what has been made, so that men are without
excuse." Romans 1:20 (NIV)

Daily Bread

Bread just won't keep, it won't stay fresh
No matter how I try,
With plastic wrap or freezer bags,
It just gets hard and dry!

The energy we need each day,
Our strength to re-employ,
Its nourishing and healthy grain
Gives life its verve and joy!

Yet regardless how I plan
To store my bread ahead,
I find my efforts futile are …
I must buy fresh instead!

Just as our life requires each day
The nourishment of bread,
So life eternal, too, must find
Strength daily in His Bread.

"I have treasured the words of his mouth
More than my daily bread." Job 23:12 (NIV)

Deadlines

Another day of sunshine,
Of shadows and of shade,
We seek some peace and quiet
Amid the life we've made.

Yet pressures forced upon us
All seem like bitter chance,
While time constraints all tell us,
We dare not stop to dance.

But Christ Himself, though busy,
Took time in each new day,
To view the tasks before Him
In true perspective's way.

He stopped, He paused, He pondered,
In all the press of life,
He spent time with His Father
No matter what the strife.

He did not rush or panic
When pressed in life's array,
Yet Scripture says He tempted was
Like we, in every way.

Sustained through all that tried Him,
In sorrow, pain and grief,

He did not doubt or question,
But held firm this belief:

The goodness of the Father
Whose ways are always sure,
Never would forsake Him
Through all He would endure!

So, as our elder Brother,
And model in this life,
Let us look to Him in all things
As we face each new day's strife.

"The Lord will guide you always; he will satisfy your needs
in a sun-scorched land and will strengthen your frame. You
will be like a well-watered garden, like a spring
whose waters never fail. Isaiah 58:11 (NIV)

Time and Task

It may seem that time moves slowly
As through life you trek along,
Then one day you wake and notice ...
Quite a lot of it is gone!

While you struggled in the moments,
Or enjoyed long days of ease,
Life itself was swiftly ebbing,
Never offering reprieve.

For the hours we've each been given
In our Father's good, wise plan,
Provide just sufficient measure
Like an hourglass trickling sand;

When the grains have sifted downward
Leaving just the empty sphere,
Signal clear thereby is given
That our time is ended here!

So, while hours full before you
Lay with tasks you still may do,
Every day with joy embrace them
With the strength He's given you!

And your life will find its meaning
As from strength to strength you go,

Ever looking unto Jesus,
For His promise tells us so!

"All the days ordained for me were written in your book before one of them came to be." Psalm 139:16 (NIV)

Stewardship

Eagerly rising at dawn's early light
Opening curtains which shut out the night,
The day to begin, new tasks to pursue,
Mind heavy with thoughts as grass is with dew.

The freshness of morning with air clear and sweet
Brings joy to the senses and strength to the feet;
To be up and doing, as poets have said,
For new work ensuing, not lying in bed.

Life holds just the measure of time deemed for us
As God's special treasure before we are dust;
So while it is day rise and welcome with joy
The work you are given your time to employ.

"So teach us to number our days
that we may get a heart of wisdom." Psalm 90:12 (ESV)

Woodside Cottage

Sitting on a hilltop
In a forest's sunny bower,
I wait in quiet wonder
As I contemplate the hour.

In the stillness of the morning
With the sound of birds so fair,
Time seems almost to stand still
In the warming summer air.

Troubles which beset all people
Today seem so far away,
And my inner inclination is
To stay right here and pray …

Spending this hour with my Savior
Who from me has never strayed,
Who through all my life's great trials
Has forever with me stayed.

Thus a bond with me He's driven,
Strong, secure and ever true,
For no matter where life called me,
Nor what it required I do,

Always my endeavors
To His caring love I brought,

And no matter what the task,
His direction always sought.

So as this day presents me
With life choices, not a few,
I desire to know His wishes
For which things He'd have me do.

Then I'll rise with zeal and fullness
In His Spirit's mighty power,
Facing gladly what life brings me
As He guides me hour by hour.

So again my life will honor Him
And testament prove true,
That "Looking unto Jesus ..."
He will always bring us through!

"'For I know the plans I have for you,' declares the Lord,
'plans to prosper you and not to harm you, plans to give
you hope and a future. Then you will call upon me and
come and pray to me, and I will listen to you. You will seek
me and find me when you seek me with all your heart.'"
Jeremiah 29:11-13 (NIV)

Morning Prayers

What is it about the morning air
That helps me meet the Savior there?
Although He's kept me through the night,
There's something about the morning light!

The eager birds all sing their song,
And urge the sun to come along
To find the joys the day will bring;
In hope they lift their voice and sing!

The pansies raise their sleepy heads
From table pots and flower beds,
Another day they gladly greet,
Reminding me my Lord to meet.

The dove, now feeding on the ground,
Untroubled by dogs' barking sound,
Still quietly focused does pursue
Food-gathering in the drying dew.

My morning mouth, now cleansed with tea,
Refreshing pallet bracing me,
I face the day with new resolve
As midnight's worries now dissolve.

While climbs the sun yet higher still,
The new day brings a strength of will

To do, to be, to love, to learn,
In all, my Father's will discern.

Someone has said a grain of sand
Reveals the world within your hand.
My garden, more than sand to me,
Shows me the Father's care daily.

His faithfulness in bringing day,
His stirring of the birds to play,
Their merry voices fill the air
Raising praises everywhere.

The tiny plantlets, flowering vines,
The pleasant palms, the towering pines,
The apple blossoms on the tree,
All reveal God's love to me.

So in the morning's early light
Before I face the day's long fight,
I gather strength in time spent there
Outside with God, in quiet prayer.

"I will bless the Lord at all times; his praise shall
continually be in my mouth. Oh, magnify the Lord
with me and let us exalt his name together!" Psalm 34:1,3 (ESV)

To Each His Work

Who gave the wren her building skill?
Through aperture so small,
As flying swiftly to the door
She pauses not at all!

She darts inside the small wren house,
Which carefully we placed,
Outside our window so to watch
Her fly from place to place.

While gathering twigs and nesting sticks
Too large to portal pass,
Who taught her how her head to turn
Sideways to put the mass

Into the little nesting house,
Where there she works inside
Close quarters, cramped, a nest
To make wherein her eggs to hide?

The artful skill and building ease
Which are to her inborn
Leave us bewildered as we seek
To replicate their form.

The gifts and skills are given to us
For work which we must do,

And building tiny nests for birds
Are not among the queue

Of tasks we're called to do each day
As on our way we go!
Rather, we fill the spot we're given
To plant and watch fruit grow.

By being just exactly that
Which we are called to be,
We thereby lift our life in praise
Now and eternally.

"O Lord, how manifold are your works! In wisdom have you
made them all; the earth is full of your creatures." Psalm 104:24 (ESV)

Glimpses of Eden

Oh the wonder of a morning
As a new day has begun,
And the birds greet with sweet singing
The brightly rising sun!

The air is fresh and clearer
Than it later will become,
When the noonday hour draws nearer
And toil's labor has begun.

Then the heat extracts its payment
For man's fall so long ago,
When our work became enslavement
On our journey here below.

But the morning makes me wonder
As each fresh new day begins,
"Does this feel like Eden's splendor
Before our first parents sinned?"

As the dew beads on the roses
And the leafy tendrils climb
Toward the light the sun exposes
On each flower, branch and vine,

So my thirsty soul looks upward
For its share of Heaven's dew,

And the strength I find in God's Word
Will again my heart renew!

"I will meditate on your precepts and fix my eyes on your ways." Psalm 119:15 (ESV)

Easter Song

I met God in the morning
When the day was at its start,
And His Presence burst like sunrise
On my dark and weary heart.

All the gloom and fear of nighttime
In one moment swept away,
By the power of His Spirit
Who sustains us every day.

Weary care dispersed in brightness,
Shattered shards His Presence swept,
As my gaze His visage held
He assured me I am kept

Safely sheltered in the promise
Of His faithful, loving care,
I need never fear nor worry
For my Father's always there.

And though storms may rage around me,
My bark threaten to o'er turn,
At the helm my Pilot guides me
To the Harbor safe from harm!

So when darkness looms before you
And you tremble on your way,

Just invite the Savior's Presence,
For He hears you when you pray.

All our fears and sin and sadness
Cannot in His Light remain,
For at Calvary He defeated death
And now forever reigns.

Conquering King, Almighty Warrior!
All sin's battles He has won!
Rejoice and trust, believer ...
For your Friend is God's dear Son!

"And behold, I am with you always, to the end of the age."
Matthew 28:20 (ESV)

Psalm for Matins

I have always loved the morning
Since my childhood's golden days,
Getting out among the flowers
Was just one of many ways

My thirsty, eager mind would there
Explore just what it meant
That from Heaven for love to save us
God's only Son was sent.

For as blossoms on the green stem,
Or as dew upon the grass,
Portends a verdant future
As through the years we pass,

So the morning holds a promise
Of the fruitful day to come,
And the energy it brings me
Musters strength to carry on;

Ever seeking in His Sonlight
Daily to pursue my toil,
'Til at last He calls me Homeward
And behind I leave earth's soil!

So I'll labor ever daily
In the promise of His Word,

And each morning ever listen
To the ways His Voice is heard.

For in giving us the daylight
After every night of rest,
He reminds us that His watchcare
And His plan for us is best.

So be strengthened, weary traveler,
As through life you daily plod …
And remember every morning,
When each day dawns, He IS God!

"Morning by morning He awakens; he awakens my ear to hear as
those who are taught." Isaiah 50:4 (ESV)

April Morning

The freshness of the morning breeze brought promise to the day,
It called me forth into the yard ... I could not stay away!
The roses, new upon their stems, all welcomed me it seemed:
This was the garden dewy, fresh, I'd visioned long in dreams

Of hearth and home and kindred dear, of pleasant days of toil,
Where joys spun through the tasks well done take root in memory's
soil,
To grow there through the passing years until a life is done,
And one looks back with thanks and praise on how it was begun.

For the dear Gardener of our lives, whose constant loving care
For flowers fresh upon their stem will nothing for them spare,
But to insure their steady growth, their fragrance, form and grace,
Has given all that's needed there to nurture them in place.

And as a flower uniquely grows with color each its own,
Our lives He tendeth steadily until we each have grown
Into the full-formed beauty He intended us to be,
Gracing Heaven's banquet table when His face at last we see.

God gives us life, and eyes to see His wonders all unfold,
To call us each to bow to Him and turn from hearts so cold.
To open, and like dewy flowers, His light and warmth receive,
Thereby to grow into full blooms if only we believe!

And yet a hardness still remains in hearts estranged from Him,
For He must touch and make them new before they can begin
The journey of a life that's sweet, that's filled with thanks and praise,
That welcomes Him like morning sun at each and every day.

Oh Lord, please grant to me this day, your tending to receive
With grateful thanks and joyful trust; You know what's best for me!
So, like the rose I gaze upon today with thankful heart,
My life will offer fragrance as with joy I do my part.

"The steadfast love of the Lord never ceases; his mercies never come
to an end; they are new every morning; great is your faithfulness."
Lamentations 3:22 (ESV)

Spring Song

Oh to capture April
For winter's long, dark night ...
The joyful, lilting bird song,
The dappled morning light,

Tree leaves young and tender,
Rose canes strong and fine,
Wisteria's graceful curtain
Draping fragrance o'er the vine,

Birds all busy nesting
Await their little brood,
Fruit trees all a'blossom
Bring promise of sweet food.

The clear, still air of morning,
Fresh and dewy from the night,
Beckons me to leave my slumber
And embrace a world of light!

"Birdeee, Birdeee, Birdeee,"
Calls the cardinal from the tree,
And he quickly hears an answer
In the game of, 'Come, catch me!'

All the world around seems bursting
With the verve and joy to sing,

For at last the winter's over!
Hope's full promise lies in Spring!

"For behold, the winter is past; the rain is over and gone.
the flowers appear on the earth, the time of singing has come,
and the voice of the turtledove is heard in our land." Song of Solomon
2:11,12 (ESV)

To A Monarch

A butterfly's a bug, you know,
Though lovelier far than most,
With colors God has given her
Which very few can boast,

As gliding through the pathless air
She stops to sip a flower,
Then taking flight, when she has supped
Refreshment for that hour,

She soars into the sunlight's gold,
Her colors catching fire!
And I am captured by the sight
And lifted from life's mire.

Her beauty has enraptured me,
It's taken me away …
For Beauty is God's gift to us
To lighten work's long day.

I stop to thank my Father
For such gifts of love He's given,
Then turn once more to tasks that wait
Not weary now, nor driven.

A sweet reminder thus I find
To help me on my way,

For I have seen a butterfly
While working here today!

"He has made everything beautiful in its time. He has also set eternity in the hearts of men; yet they cannot fathom what God has done from beginning to end." Ecclesiastes 3:11 (NIV)

Be Prepared

You're going to be tired
At the end of the day ...
How will you spend
Your time on the way?

Will you walk with the knowledge
Your life's in His Hand?
Will you give Him each day
For the work He has planned?

How will you invest
All the days you are given
As you travel through life
'til at last you reach Heaven?

Some moments are quiet,
Some days filled with pain,
And some days are blest
With love's sweet refrain.

Others seem hurried
As new needs arise,
Those days turn our eyes
Away from the prize;

That high Calling fair
To which we were drawn,

When first we encountered
God's beloved Son.

How will you correct
Your course in the fray
Of life's heated battles
You meet on the way?

What resource or strength
Will serve your needs well
As you face the powers
And darkness of Hell?

For daily we struggle
And toil on our way …
We have not yet come
To Eternity's Day!

And as we face giants
We meet on the road,
Our burdens encumber
Our fight with their load.

Lord! Help us! Please guide us
And give us Your power!
Our own strength is useless
In trouble's dark hour.

Each day give us wisdom
And draw us to You,
To focus Your purpose
For life in clear view.

Give hearts that reach outward
And hands quick to serve,
Give courage and strength;
Renew zeal and verve!

So when each day is over
And we rest our head,
Your joy will accompany
Us to our bed,

Just knowing You've led us
In all we have done,
And You'll bring a new day
With the rising sun.

Then as we journey on
Through this voyage of life,
Your call will sustain us
In all of its strife.

When at last we shall hear
Your glad, "Child, welcome Home!",
Our life-song will praise bring
Before Your bright throne!

"Finally, be strong in the Lord and in the strength of his might.
Put on the whole armor of God, that you may be able to stand
against the schemes of the devil." Ephesians 6:10,11 (ESV)

Victory in Jesus

Please don't think I have it easy
As through this life I go ...
Don't assume I have no struggles
Just because it doesn't show.

For great depths of sin and sadness
Into every life appear,
As we labor on our journey
Up to Heaven from down here.

But our Savior true has blessed us
With great measures of His grace,
As His Spirit guards and keeps us
Every step along this race.

Since Christ traveled here before us,
As on earth He really lived,
For our troubles and temptations
His great strength and power He gives!

So, no matter the affliction
Or the difficulty sore,
Just remember; Call on Jesus!
He stands ready at the door

To sustain your weary spirit
As you toil along the way,

Every step He's there beside you
'til you reach that perfect day.

For this life will soon be over,
Now our victory's in full view …
Jesus died, yet lives to keep us
In everything we do!

His help is never ending,
His power has no bounds,
His love has won the battle,
And all praise to Him resounds!

"Many are the afflictions of the righteous, but the
Lord delivers him out of them all." Psalm 34:19 (ESV)

The Strength of An Old Oak Tree

(Annoso Robore Quercus)

It takes a long time
For an oak tree to grow,
Through Summer's sun
and Winter's snow,

The weather blows
And beats about,
Growing the sapling
Strong and stout.

Branches reach upward
Toward rain and light,
As roots plunge deep
In soil's quiet night.

Seasons' years
Add ring on ring,
Birds build nests
From which to sing.

Leaves that bud
Grow old and fall
To warm the ground
When snow cloaks all.

A lesson there
For all to see
Who closely observe
The growing tree;

The things which seem
So harsh and bare
Produce the strength
And growth so fair.

God's purpose and
Design, we know,
Will strengthen us
And make us grow.

So when winds push,
And hard you lean,
Recall the sapling,
Tender, green;

The storms will only
Stronger make,
For young trees, supple
Will bend, not break,

And as roots deeper
Grow in the ground,
The tree with old age
Will be crowned!

"...to give them a beautiful headdress instead of ashes, the oil of gladness instead of mourning, the garment of praise instead of a faint spirit; that they may be called oaks of righteousness, the planting of the Lord that he may be glorified." Isaiah 61:3 (ESV)

Landscape Painting

The morning light dispels the night
Like Monet's garden green;
As each new waking greets my eye
The dappled shadows seem

To sing with joy and call me forth
Into life's moving stream,
Where there awaits some work for me
Which ne'er before has been.

A fresh new start, time to begin
To ply my brush with care,
To capture all the shades and hues
Of color hidden there.

That on the palette of my life
The Master's touch will be
So clearly painted, deeply writ,
That passersby can see.

For all the days He gives to us
Are trusted to our care,
His praise to raise, His plan to find
In all that's painted there.

Take up your brush with each new day,
Begin with joy and verve!

The Master holds your life in His,
It's not up to your nerve.

He has not called for solo flights,
Nor grave requirements given,
But promised comfort in our nights
Though tempest-tossed and driven.

What e'er our story here on earth,
What e'er the call may be,
The Master Painter, brush in hand,
Paints ever faithfully.

To the large canvas of His Plan
He calls us to attend,
And paint with Him the strokes He's planned
Until we reach our end.

Then joyfully He'll take us Home
Forever there to be;
In great museums of His love
His Masterworks we'll see!

"for it is God who works in you, both to will and to
work for his good pleasure." Philippians 2:13 (ESV)

A Reminder

Today I found a bird's egg,
Or rather, just a shell …
Empty it was and broken
By the height from which it fell.

No chance to live and grow wings
Nor through clear air to soar,
The tiny life that started
Was cut short forevermore.

The sadness which came o'er me
As I held the shell in hand
Reminded me again …
In this life we cannot stand

Upon some lofty ideal
Of a perfect world of bliss,
For sin's stain has tainted all things,
And perfection's now amiss.

So the little eggshell brought me
Starkly to this world's demise.
As I held the fragment gently
And looked up to search the skies

For a nest, or watching parent,
Hidden high up in the tree …

But no sign of either met me
Though I searched most carefully.

Just the tiny blue reminder
Of a life that might have been
Turned my thoughts to our dear Father
And the true life we've been given.

Through the wonder of His Son's life
And His death which took our sin,
We now have hope's true promise
As a new life we begin.

Beyond the earthly limits
Of this realm of time and space ...
Someday we'll really see God,
Really look upon His face!

Then the shadows, fears and dangers,
Which with sadness fill our days,
Will be gone, and just dim memory
Will give cause to sing God's praise.

So, when you see a token
Which reminds you of sin's toll,
Let it point you to the Savior,
And be thankful Earth's not all.

For a better world is coming
With no sorrow, sin or blight,
When God reigns in hearts eternal
With no further need to fight.

So I thank You, Heavenly Father,
For Your gift to me today,
Of a tiny bird shell fragment
Which brought my thoughts this way.

"Incline your ear and hear the words of the wise,
and apply your heart to my knowledge, that your trust
may be in the Lord." Proverbs 22:17,19 (ESV)

Lesson From A Pansy

The pansy is a sturdy plant
Though beaten down by rain,
When sunshine warms the ground beneath ...
It blooms with flowers again!

The hailstorm, which with thunderous noise
Awakened me last night,
The pansies, sleeping in their beds,
Tore ragged with its might.

In grief I saw my garden fair
Reduced to shreds and snarls;
All the dear flowers I'd planted there
Through many toiling hours

Were only now small, muddy smears
Upon the soggy soil;
It seemed the labor I had spent
Was merely wasted toil.

And yet, as sunlight bright shines down
Through heaven's now clear sky,
Something in the pansies tell me
They refuse to die.

Though beaten down among the clods
Of darkly sodden earth,

They bravely raise their weary heads
To joy in a new birth.

Lord! Let me more like pansies be
When trouble weighs me down,
To ever lift my face to you ...
The Sonlight Who came down!

"Again Jesus spoke to them saying,
'I am the light of the world. Whoever
follows me will not walk in darkness
but will have the light of life.' " John 8:12 (ESV)

Requiem

Colors, flowers, beautiful words, and music to fill the air,
Mountain streams, fluttering birds, and tall trees everywhere,
The grandeur of the stars, the splendor of the night,
The warmth of the sun, the radiance of light,

The year's steady passing through each season's song,
The days of our life growing character strong,
The joy of new friendship, the comfort of old,
The promise of Heaven when our tale is told,

All these keep us going through moments of life,
Through times of deep sorrow, great conflict and strife.
For this world is broken, the end soon will come,
Our Savior will call us, our work will be done.

The labor which daily our life doth extract
Will cease to be toilsome … we'll then be intact
With God's one great purpose for which all was made,
And sin's heavy burden will finally be laid

To rest once for all, and our joy will increase;
At Calvary Christ conquered death with His sweet Peace!
Thus days which await us in Heaven so fair,
Will have not sins' limits which weigh us down here.

"My times are in your hand; rescue me from the hand of my
enemies and from my persecutors!" Psalm 31:15 (ESV)

Lodestone

Are you living in the rhythm of your life,
Husband, father, mother, daughter, son or wife?
For each day that comes and goes
And your story longer grows,
Is it one of happy joy or weary strife?

Do you know who you are
As life daily you pace?
Do you have a North Star
Guiding you to your place?

Does the anxious stress of care
Make the burden that you bear
Overwhelm your heart
With thoughts that life's not fair?

Do the folks you pass each day
Pose a problem, or a way
For the Savior to extend
On earth His stay?

In the eyes of those you meet
Do you there your Savior greet,
Serving them as did our Lord
When washing feet?

Are you joining God's great symphony
Or part of sin's cacophony
As you daily journey
On this road called life?

Do the words you speak each day
Over others hold a sway
Of love's kindly peacefulness,
Or fractious strife?

For in this world's dust and grime,
We each have enough time
To complete the path He's given
As we climb ...

Ever upward on the way,
As He guides us day by day,
'Til we there arrive at last
And with Him stay.

"We have this sure and steadfast anchor of the soul, a hope that
enters into the inner place behind the curtain, where Jesus has gone
as a forerunner on our behalf, having become a high priest forever
after the order of Melchizedek." Hebrews 6:19,20 (ESV)

Harvest

In youth I thought life would be moments
Through hours you had carefully planned ...
Now I can say,
As I've live day by day,
Life's THIS moment you hold in your hand!

The Word, which still speaks through the ages,
And calls us to focus on Him,
Reminds us each day
In words that we pray,
Our life is to be His sweet hymn.

Those daily tasks and obligations
Which sometimes feel burdensome, sore,
Are ways which we praise
As voices we raise,
And look to His strength evermore.

So keep your eyes focused before you,
Look well at the task you must do,
It's in things well done
The Father, and Son,
And Spirit will make your life new.

It's today, not the future, that matters;
This moment's been given to use,
In blessing and praise

To lift and to raise
His Name before all watching you.

So lean on His strength in your doing,
Never forget that He cares,
And a life blessed with joy
As His strength you employ
Will lighten the load that you bear.

"For this reason I bow my knees before the Father, from whom every family in heaven and on earth is named, that according to the riches of his glory he may grant you to be strengthened with power through his Spirit in your inner being." Ephesians 3:15,16 (ESV)

East Window

The East window in the morning's
Where I meet the Lord each day;
As light streams across my Bible
I take moments there to pray,

Offering to our good, wise Father
All the thoughts that trouble me,
Trusting ever in His promise
He the Rock to me will be.

Nighttime's short and fretful passage
Brought me weary to this day,
And it stretches out before me
Holding stress along the way.

So, dear Lord, I need Your power,
Strength and courage all to bear
Tasks and duties which await me
As I rise up from my chair.

For alone I cannot carry
All I see which must be done,
When the morning turns to midday
'Neath the hot and rising sun.

Thus these moments here before You
On my knees I gladly spend,

Knowing you will hear and answer,
For You have called me friend!

"No longer do I call you servants, for the servant does not know what his master is doing; but I have called you friends, for all that I have heard from my Father I have made known to you." John 15:15 (ESV)

The Monarch

A butterfly lay dying
Upon the garden soil,
His summer life now ended,
Now done his days of toil.

The russet of his wing span
As fluttering there he lay,
With shades of Autumn stirring,
Called me forth to face my day.

For time moves swiftly onward
Through all our span of life,
Like him, we'll soon lie dying,
Finished all our work and strife.

Though valiantly he struggled
His wings to spread once more,
As all the while I watched him
From out my kitchen door,

His story now was ending,
No flower will feel his touch,
No child delight in wonder
That God would care so much

About our life to bring us
The Monarch's colors rare,

For now his time was over,
And he was dying there.

So Lord, in all the lessons
You show us every day,
Help us our days to number ...
We have not long to stay.

The color and the beauty
You've given us to share,
Has but a measured moment
Of time you've give here.

We, too, shall soon lie dying
Upon this earth You've made,
Our story here be ended,
Our glory dimmed in shade.

Yet now our wings stretch upward!
There's work we still can do,
And through our life of color
Bring joy and honor You;

A blessing be to others
As they observe our flight,
While pointing them to You, Lord,
Before our own last night.

Then we shall enter Heaven,
Your beauty to adore,
And new wings then spread outward ...
Eternity explore!

"The years of our life are seventy, or even by reason of strength eighty; yet their span is but toil and trouble. They are soon gone, and we fly away. So teach us to number our days that we may get a heart of wisdom." Psalm 90:10,12 (ESV)

The Sentinel

The pine stands watching every day
In sun's light gold or storm's dark gray,
And, listening, hears what birdies say.

The quiet sentinel, 'neath whose guard
Small folk feed safely in the yard,
With tales could rival any bard.

For through long years the passing scene
He's witnessed, as his needles green
Have small lives sheltered, safe, unseen.

The years marched forward in advance
While creatures, as though in a trance,
Were guided through their lifetime's dance.

Still today the pine remains,
His trunk has born the seasons' strains
Through drought years and abundant rains,

It has endured, reminder tall,
That life is more than moment small,
And God's big picture trumps man's Fall.

And though we all see hardships drear
Which bring us doubt and cause us fear,
The pine reminds, "Your God is near!"

Through all life's storms, all kinds of weather,
He has put our heads together ...
Reminding us we're in His tether,

Surely bound through all our days
In Livings' bundle we shall raise
Through all our life unending praise.

And like the pine, so tall and straight,
Enduring, we fear not the wait.
For our Guard stands at Heaven's Gate,

Our call to answer, path to guide,
He's promised to stay by our side
And 'neath His shade we can abide,

Protected by Love's sheltering,
So on our path we, too, can sing,
And like the small birds praise the King!

"Even though someone is pursuing you to take your life,
the life of my master will be bound securely in the bundle
of the living by the Lord your God." I Samuel 25:29 (NIV)

Through Wildfire Haze

A feather fell from a mourning dove
As I sat outside, floating down from above,
Reminding once more of my Father's kind care,
For feathers are numbered, as surely as hair.

Through morning light, haze-filled
By wildfire's brown smoke,
A gentle breeze brought me
The feather which spoke

To my heart, writ large,
As I pondered my day,
Wondering just what good words
I would hear my Lord say?

Then while I was sitting
In my chair outside,
The gray feather brought words
For which I had cried.

A strong, true reminder
Of our Father's care,
Its brief witness told me,
"There's nothing to fear!"

The Lord, our Creator,
Still reigns above all,

And what we do here cannot
His Plan forestall.

That glad day He promised
Will one day dawn clear,
In bright, smokeless Light
His dear face will appear!

"Are not two sparrows sold for a penny? Yet not one of them will
fall to the ground apart from the will of your Father. And even the
very hairs of your head are all numbered. So don't be afraid;
you are worth more than many sparrows." Matthew 10:29-31 (NIV)

Disappointment

"It's nothing like the manual,"
He said, with sadness in his voice,
And yet there's still so much in life
For which we can rejoice;

The daily tasks which occupy
Our energy and time
Give reasons and occasions
To exhibit Truth sublime.

Our expectations, hopes and dreams,
Envisioned when we're young,
Still give us drive and fortitude
For plans we have begun.

Our Father knows how frail our frame,
Our weakness, too, He knows,
And throughout all life's weary years
His grace and love bestows.

So look above when life bears down
And weighs you with its care,
Rejoice in hope! Look up in faith!
Believe His Word so fair.

He will not fail, though we may fall,
His Truth will stand secure;

Its anchored in His character,
And so we can be sure

He will accomplish all He's planned
In giving us this life.
Nothing can thwart our certain good,
Regardless of the strife!

So be alert to all He has,
And watch with careful gaze
To see His Plan unfold for you
Throughout life's seeming maze.

You see, the "Manual" which we read
Must be His Word so true,
For any other book or plan
Just simply will not do.

Only in His Word laid bare
Our sinful self and need,
Only on His work alone
Sufficient faith we feed.

"Your word is a lamp to my feet and a light to my path." Psalm 119:105
(ESV)

Vesper Song

I sat out until the sun set
On my garden's lovely scene,
Watching all the birds that gathered
On the leafy branches green.

The bright morning light had faded
To a softer, paler hue,
And the birdsongs, once so brilliant,
In this light were softer too.

Their joyful calls had carried
This world through another day,
Now in vesper tones they called me
To stop my work … and pray,

Joining them to thank our Father
For this day's tender care,
Strength from food, shelter's safety,
And needed clothes to wear.

So I paused a quiet moment,
Stilled my heart to thank and pray,
And I joined the birds' sweet vesper
At the closing of the day.

"Let my prayer be counted as incense before you, and
the lifting up of my hands as the evening sacrifice!" Psalm 141:2 (ESV)

Sweet Hour of Prayer

There's always more to pray about
Than you have time to pray ...
But never let that keep you,
At the closing of the day,

With no thought or word to utter
For you did not find a way
To address your Heavenly Father,
Or a proper phrase to say.

He longs for you to seek Him,
And full ready He is made,
By the purchase of your pardon;
So you need not be afraid!

Boldly come into His Presence,
As the Spirit gives you aid,
Let your heart pour out its anguish
For your debt of sin is paid!

Spend some time in quiet wonder
And reflect upon His grace;
Remember how He loves you ...
Seek to live before His face.

So the day you hear His summons
That no longer you must race,

Gladly you will meet your Savior
There in Heaven's glorious place!

"Do not be anxious about anything, but in
everything by prayer and supplication with
thanksgiving let your requests be made known
to God." Philippians 4:6 (ESV)

Making New Friends

Moving means no friends, you see,
Which opens challenges for me;
The need for others is so strong
I have to take risks to belong!

So as I dwell in places new
The thing I find I have to do
Is reach out, be kind, to those I meet,
Like neighbors living on my street;

To open wide my heart's closed door
Then friendships in my life will pour.
Make room, spread wide, increase the space,
Allow new folks to fill the place

Which now lies barren, cold, alone …
Instead, to others become known.
For as the Word of old has said,
We need each other here to tread

The path of life where'er we go
As on we travel here below,
And hand-in-hand the journey make,
Whate're the road our lives may take.

Our stories here then linked will be
And live on through Eternity

When we arrive at Heaven's door
To dwell together evermore.

In friendship sweet, God's Family one,
When all our stories here are done,
True joy complete then will be ours,
Forever free from sin's dark powers

"Enlarge the place of your tent, and let the curtains of your habitation be stretched out; do not hold back; lengthen your cords and strengthen your stakes." Isaiah 54:2 (ESV)

Building A Home

The beauty of a home comes from
The life that's lived within,
Whether cot on quiet hillside,
Or loft high above the din,

Or farm spread across wide acres,
Or sprawling, grand estate,
Cozy cabin in the mountains,
Rustic cottage by the lake.

All these have one thing in common
Which is sought by every man …
A place to go when weary,
A place to live God's plan.

The walls and roof protecting
The lives that dwell inside,
A shelter from the weather
Where warm family ties abide,

And memories of loved ones,
Their joys and sorrows shared,
Hallow the sanctuary
Reminding us we cared.

Foreshadowing a future where
Our joys will be complete,

When our Heavenly Home will greet us
And our Savior we shall meet.

There the beauty we desire
In the lives we're building here
Will shine perfect when the fire,
Dross removing, makes things clear.

So in seeking earthly dwellings
Be reminded of one thought ...
All which here seems so enduring
Will one Day be rendered naught.

For all things which here are soiled
Will be changed to be no more,
And the life we've lived here hallowed
Will be where the gold is stored.

Every building we've erected
Which has housed our life within
Will be gladly then forgotten
As we leave behind all sin.

The ideal of home and hearthside
Which has colored all our schemes
Will be realized in Heaven's Light
And fulfill our fondest dreams.

So be patient as you live here
On this side of Heaven's shore,
Live your life within His wise care
And your Home will be secure!

For He's promised He will keep you

No matter where you dwell,
And each house you live in here
Will be adequate as well.

Therefore, focus on the quality
Of life you live each day,
Blessing those who live around you,
Sharing strength along the way.

"By wisdom a house is built, and by understanding
it is established; by knowledge the rooms are filled
with all precious and pleasant riches." Proverbs 24:3,4 (ESV)

Autumn Anthem

Just when I least expected,
Wasn't planning it at all,
Looking out onto my garden
Trees cast shadows long and tall.

Morning air was clearly different,
Skies above were bluer too,
As the equinox approached
Plants all donned a softer hue.

Fall was just around the corner,
Summer's day was at a close,
All of nature seemed now ready
For her time of deep repose.

Through the sorter days that follow,
Bringing chiller winds and ice,
Plant roots sleep in loamy soil
To escape cold winter's vice.

Lord, as I reflect on Autumn
And the days for me You've planned,
Tune my heart to Your sweet music,
Make me ready, strong to stand

Through the chilling winds of winter,
Which unto my life must come

In the days You have before me,
'til at last You call me Home.

Give me strength and peace and courage
To face all the cold life brings,
Knowing through it all You're with me,
I'll rest safe upon Your wings.

As You bear me up and carry
All the load of heavy toil,
Though my leaves all fall and wither,
I'll be rooted in Your soil!

That strong, earthy Word You've given,
Which brings nourishment and peace,
Will enable me to live on
'til from winter I'm released

Then with blossoms far more lovely
That I've known through this dark night,
I'll grow in Your courts forever
In Your glorious, warm, sweet Light!

"But I trust in you, O Lord; I say, 'You are my
God.' My times are in your hand." Psalm 31:14,15 (ESV)

Diligence

Leafy shadows leaving,
Longer days now gone;
Autumn's fast approaching,
Stilling summer's song,

Turning our thoughts inward,
Calling us indoors,
Gathering our kindred,
Sharing winter's stores.

Then we'll laugh and savor
All we've laid aside,
And, in the midst of winter,
Find we can abide.

Then what may come before us,
Even as the cold grows strong,
Will matter not, for to us
Night will never still the song

Of all the stores we've laid by
For the chill of night ...
Those joys and hopes we're saving
Until the time is right.

Through snow, or sleet, or shadow,
Or howling winds that roar,

We'll have no fear of want, for
We've all we need and more!

"Go to the ant ... consider her ways, and
be wise ... she prepares her bread in summer
and gathers her food in harvest." Proverbs 6:6,8 (ESV)

A Song of the Seasons

An acorn fell upon my path …
I held it in my morning grasp,
A sign that fall was on the way,
That summer had not long to stay.

The neighborhood's deserted now,
Just quiet fills the air;
The people have gone elsewhere …
There's simply no one here!

For knowing chilling winter
Will soon be here to stay,
They're all out traveling seeking
Just one last chance to play.

Before harsh winds of winter
Will keep them all indoors,
(Except for all the children
Whose feet track snow on floors.)

Then fireplaces' bright blazing
Will cheer the families' night,
While thoughts of Christmas coming
Will set their hearts alight!

For God has given Jesus
To strengthen our weak hope

And fill our life with promise ...
We need not simply cope!

When through this world we journey
Reflecting on His Song,
No winter, how e'er bitter,
Can chill our heart for long.

His promise of spring's coming
Brings joy to every day;
We know His Word is valid,
He won't stay long away.

But soon, like bursting blossoms,
His Spring will fill the air,
As to new realms He calls us
To live forever there.

Where winter's chill, a memory,
We never will recall,
His Light will warm and cheer us
Beyond this world's dark Fall.

"And God said, 'Let there be lights in the
expanse of the heavens to separate the day from
the night. And let them be for signs and for seasons,
And for days and for years.' " Genesis 1:14 (ESV)

Autumnal Equinox

The roses woke to autumn's air,
No breeze disturbed their quiet stare.
Long shadows shade the leaf-strewn yard,
No insect near, no need to guard.

Along the fence a squirrel appears,
Busy gathering without fear
The birdseed left for passing friends,
Who to our yard their way will wend,

As onward to the South they fly,
To feeder dipping from the sky.
The sunlight casts a different hue,
And thus more slowly dries the dew.

So, grass blades sparkle, tree leaves drip,
Providing drinks for birds to sip;
Yet none appear, the air is still,
No leaf stirs at my windowsill.

For autumn bears a stately grace
And dignity in every place;
Her Majesty paused in quiet repose,
Reflecting on the coming snows,

When winter breaks upon the scene
And white replaces all that's green;

When time is short for light is gone,
And, with it, summer's noisy song.

My childhood memory's bold relief
Positions central without grief;
Those younger days, now auld lang syne,
When life before me stretched in time,

And autumn harkened school's return
With lessons eagerly to learn,
A season bold with studies bright
To busy me through winter's night.

So, in this time of autumn's rest,
May we, too, take some time to test
The work in summer we have done,
And joyful, offer to the Son

Our labored fruits for His dear gaze,
And lift them up to Him in praise
For strength and skills which He has given;
He is our Source, both here and heaven!

"Let the favor of the Lord our God be upon us, and establish
the work of our hands upon us; yes, establish the work of
our hands." Psalm 90:17 (ESV)

Shadows Lengthen

Across the lawn and patio
The shadows lengthen fast ...
Summer's waning now, you see,
Her days of play are past.

Now Fall awaits her entry glad
In colors' brighter hue,
To signal time is fleeting and
There's work for us to do!

Our lives we've spent deciding
Just what tasks required our time,
And now we realize each day
Has limits, though sublime.

Our Summer now is over
And time still moves along ...
While work ahead requires of us
To ever journey on.

Upon the path the wheels of time
Will carry us ahead,
Accomplishing those very tasks
For which our lives were bred.

So, Lord, please keep us looking up,
Dependent on Your care,
We ask no other benefit

Than Your kind Presence there

To comfort and sustain our future days,
Like paths we've trod …
To guide the Winter days ahead,
For You alone are God!

And all the trust You've given us,
Things placed within our care,
We offer daily back to You
For Your good purpose here.

Please use us, Lord, in Your good plan,
To glorify and bless
Your Name as through our very lives
Your goodness we confess.

And on that day You take us Home
And we then see Your face,
We pray our time of being here
Has left a better place

For those who follow in our wake
To gather strength and trust,
Acknowledging Your goodness great,
That Man is more than dust;

For purpose high and lofty
Every one of us was made,
Your praise to bring eternally
Through Life that will not fade.

"The Lord will fulfill His purpose for me; your steadfast love,
O Lord, endures forever." Psalm 138:8 (ESV)

Squirrel Terrace

I sit and watch the squirrels at play
Each morning when I rise,
Upon my doorstep they await
With hunger in their eyes.

The braver ones familiar are
With treats and nuts I give,
They come expectantly each day
For food they need to live.

A pattern and a rhythm now
Established I have made
To help sustain their little ones
Who wait in nests of shade.

In long days past, in other climes,
Racoons received our fare,
And now God's creatures, furry brown,
In this place all come near.

A cheeky robin strides across
The terrace's tiled floor,
Inspecting where the squirrels have been
In hopes of finding more.

But not a single crumb remains
Of what I've scattered there,

The busy squirrels have taken all
With nothing left to spare.

Because the coming Winter harsh
Keeps them all gathering stores,
For to survive the long, cold months
Requires enormous hordes.

So I will keep on feeding them,
My little squirrel friends,
No pets have we to tend and feed
Through our life's transient trends.

But God has given animals
Mankind to cheer and aid,
And as we watch their pace of life
We are much less afraid;

For as the seasons come and go
And daily life's supplied,
Our Father has assured us all
He ever is our Guide,

Sustaining us through all the days
We live upon this earth,
'Til, in His time, He takes us Home
Where there will be no death.

So thanks we raise, and praises, too,
For His great love and care …
No matter what the seasons bring,
We know He's always there!

"Godliness with contentment is great gain." I Timothy 6:8 (NIV)

Night Watches

Once more the darkness settles in
As night enrobes the sky,
Replacing all our anxious thoughts
With sweet sleep's lullaby.

The day of toil has ended now,
We seek strength to renew,
As, through the wee hours slumbering,
We grasp a broader view.

For in our times of deepest sleep
The Holy Spirit, hovering near,
Reminds us of our Father's love
And of our Savior Brother dear

Who promised not to leave us
Without comfort, or alone,
But sent His Holy Spirit,
As He stands before the Throne

Ever interceding for us,
To the Father takes our part,
Claiming for us Calvary's merit,
Giving us a brand new start!

So to rest with joy and gladness
And deep slumber swiftly go ...

Knowing through the long night watches
He stands guardian o'er your soul.

"He will not let your foot be moved; he who keeps you
will not slumber. Behold, he who keeps Israel will neither
slumber nor sleep." Psalm 121:3,4 (ESV)

First Frost

Ice crystals reflecting
The sun's early light
Reveal all the frost
That formed through the night.

In stillness the morning
Gives birth to the day
When sunshine will melt
All the hoarfrost away.

But just in this moment,
As I step outside,
The vastness and beauty
Of winter presides

O'er all the yard's herbage ...
Each plant and each tree,
With grand, pristine whiteness
And jeweled dignity

To rival earth's monarchs
In palaces fair.
(With displays of nature,
Crown jewels can't compare!)

And as I turn inward,
Still kept in the light,

My thoughts turn to You, Lord,
And Your plan so right.

For just as the cold night
Of winter brings frost,
Our life holds its moments
Of deep chill and loss.

And yet when your Sonlight
Dawns bright on the scene,
Through the chill and the loss
Your fair beauty is seen,

As reflections of grace shine
Through all of our days,
Life responds with bright sparkle
When we give you praise.

So Lord, keep us mindful
In all that we do;
No matter the trial,
To keep praising You!

"In all their affliction he was afflicted, and the
angel of his presence saved them; in his love
and in his pity he redeemed them; he lifted
them up and carried them all the days of old."
Isaiah 63:9 (ESV)

Standard Time

The equinox has come and gone,
Fair autumn's here to stay;
Tomorrow brings November's
One less hour of sunny day.

"The clocks fall back," the signs all said,
We're ending summer's play.
So now we settle down again
To rest, and while away

The longer hours as winter nears
And brings his share of cold;
To venture forth and run about
We will not be so bold.

But seeking home and hearthside ease,
We'll eat, and drink, and read,
We'll plan ahead for springtime days
And talk of planting seed

Which blossoms bright and tasty fruit
The summer season brings,
As days again grow longer
And the birds return to sing.

So as we contemplate the days
Of quiet and of dark,

Lord, keep us ever mindful ...
You alone are life's true spark!

Seasons which to us bring change
And cause us to reflect,
Are gifts you've given freely
To our lives, which you respect.

For to each they bring occasion
To be thankful and lift praise
To You for your kind wisdom
In creating all our days.

"From the rising of the sun to its setting,
the name of the Lord is to be praised!" Psalm 113:3 (ESV)

Evensong

I love homey, winter evenings,
When thoughts turn to cozy themes,
And hearts long for love's warm touch
To rekindle fading dreams.

The candle's glow which draws us
From a day of weary care,
Reminds with warm light flickering,
Hope is always there!

No matter how the day went,
What troubles posed a threat,
The evening brings a respite,
And time to heal regret.

A cup of tea stands ready
To lend its soothing bit,
And tender, buttery toast points
Bring us comfort as we sit

Discussing all the happenings
And commerce of the day,
Places where our skills and talents
All were offered in the fray.

For each day has its own calling,
Each engaging us to try,

To bring some truth and beauty
To those whom we pass by.

And as the evening gathers
Night's shawl around her form,
Our family comes together
In a house that's safe and warm

To spend some time reflecting
On all the day has been
Before sleep comes, for bright dawn
Will soon beckon us again.

"In peace I will both lie down and sleep; for you
alone, O Lord, make me dwell in safety." Psalm 4:8 (NIV)

Thanksgiving Eve

Those things we thought important were,
And labored all our days,
Now, looking back, are just a blur
Fast-fading in the haze.

For life has moved us all along
The path we chose and trod,
The question now, which looming large,
Is, "Did we honor God?"

Were days of toil spent needlessly
Pursuing trivial ends?
Or did my goal and focus lead
Me helping hands to lend

To fellow travelers on the road
Who stumbled on their way?
Was I there for them in their need
To brighten their dark day?

For life is built of moments
And we're given just a few,
To help and touch another
In the daily things we do.

So as the shadows lengthen
And our day on earth is done,

Others will follow after
In paths we have begun.

Will they find steady footprints,
Those which we safely trod
Through life, which lead them upward
Connecting them to God?

Dear Lord! Please stretch my vision,
My focus stay on You,
In everything be honored
In all I say and do.

So in the days remaining
As life on earth I live,
Please keep my arms wide open
To others help to give.

As You have given all things
Sufficient for Your Call,
Let me rejoice as daily,
"I surrender all,"

Remembering that my life
Itself is Your great gift.
And all I have and treasure
To You I'm called to lift

In praise and adoration
For everything You Are,
My caring, loving Father,
Who's called me from afar

To walk with You in service,
To be Christ's hands and feet,
To live in Love's compassion
Toward everyone I meet.

And then, when glancing backward,
As life's days here are gone,
I'll joy in Your bright Presence
And hear You say, "Well done!"

"Ponder the path of your feet; then all your ways will be sure." Proverbs 4:26 (ESV)

Advent Once Again

Again we start the Christian year
Recalling our Lord did appear,
In Bethlehem one winter's day,
Laid in a manger filled with hay.

And soon we'll celebrate His birth,
That wondrous Child Who came to earth,
Who, born to die, rose from the dead,
Now reigns in Heaven, our Living Head!

He promised He would soon return,
And through His Word we also learn,
He comes again in glorious power
To fully bring that peace to flower,

For which our waiting longing yearns,
As through another year earth turns.
So now we welcome Him with joy,
And gladsome praise our tongues employ!

"The people who walked in darkness have seen
a great light; those who dwelt in the land of deep
darkness, on them has the light shined." Isaiah 9:2 (ESV)

Advent Solace

How brightly blooms my Christmas rose
Today, long before snow,
As brightly bloomed The Christmas Rose
That day so long ago.

Blood red and fresh it greets the day
Against the fence so drab,
As Christ our Savior met each day
Before laid on grave's slab.

My weary heart its red inspired
To garner strength anew,
Though I had wakened stiff and tired,
This day I can get through!

For toil and tears attend my way
And strength will soon be gone,
But for today with Christ close by,
I'll work with joy and song!

For as the red rose vibrant blooms
Inspiring all who see,
So Christ's love fills my heart with hope
And joy, whate'er may be

Awaiting in the days ahead
As through this life I go,

When seeking Him, my daily trek
Will upward be, though slow.

Until at last He calls me Home
To dwell with Him on high,
Where angel song still loudly rings
Into the world's dark sky.

And I shall then be gathered there
With loved ones now long gone,
To join with angels singing praise
To God in endless song!

"Creation itself will be liberated from its bondage to decay and brought into the glorious freedom of the children of God." Romans 8:21 (NIV)

Shepherds' Advent Joy

The roses froze, the sky was gray,
The sun shone not the whole short day.
The droplets, from the sprinkler born,
Had frozen hard as field-dried corn.

The garden bare and lifeless lay,
With leaves all strewn in disarray.
My winter heart felt sad indeed,
For fruit was gone from planted seed.

A barren time without the cheer
And fellowship of loved ones dear,
As Christmas Day approaching came,
I saw this year was not the same;

No parties bright with friends who care
These special days and joys to share,
No homeward treks with presents brought
By those whose memory now I sought.

The customs and traditions past
On which I'd worked, in hopes to last,
Were now abandoned ... left unpacked,
For days' short hours around the track

Of this world's journey past the sun
Had left my energy undone.

And hours which the brief daylight gave
Were used in other, mundane ways.

Lord! Give my heart a touch from Thee!
Lighten with joy my Advent plea!
I long to in Your Presence wait,
As shepherds lingered at the gate

Before your bright Nativity,
And lift my voice in praise to Thee!
For You Alone are winter's Light!
You Alone make darkness Bright!

As in this world, so cloaked in night,
Your Spirit broods and guides to Right
Until at last all night shall cease,
Until at last You bring Your peace!

Our own devices poor we bring,
We offer all to Christ, our King!
We cannot our own fires ignite …
We cannot brighten earth's dark night!

Oh Christ! Be born in us each day
As we awake and wend our way
Across this world's long journey wide …
Until the day we're at Your side.

"Again Jesus spoke to them saying, 'I am the light of the world.
Whoever follows me will not walk in darkness, but will have the
light of life." John 8:12 (ESV)

Joy to the World

The flat gray of the morning
Robbed my heart of joy's desire ...
Then it happened! Unexpected!
And my spirit caught on fire!

For a cardinal's glorious red inflamed
The bare branch of the tree,
And my heart rejoiced with gladness
When his color I did see!

For the morning gray made contrast,
Like a palette, for his flight,
And the joy his song encoded
Made the day both fair and bright.

Banished was the gray of morning ...
Banished, too, my dreary night,
As his joyous song and color
Filled my soul with new delight!

Lord, one thing I ask be given
As I journey through this life;
Let me ever see Your color,
Hear Your song amid the strife.

For my spirit does get weary
As I see the gray of sin,

And I recognize the drabness
In my heart so deep within.

Keep me focused on the blessed,
Blood-red color of Your Gift …
Let me hear Your Spirit's singing
In my soul, which then will lift

The gray burden, dank and dreary,
Which this world around me bears,
Answers bringing the great query,
Thus relieving strain of cares.

For Your purposes are larger
Than the palette which we see,
And Your Plan for us can only
Be revealed on bended knee.

So dear Lord, please guide and keep us
As we journey this life long,
Keep our eyes on Jesus focused,
Place into our hearts His Song!

"Oh the depth of the riches and wisdom and knowledge of
God! How unsearchable are his judgments and how inscrutable
His ways. For from him and through him and to him are all things.
To him be glory forever. Amen." Romans 11:33,36 (ESV)

The Ending of the Year

Christmas has now come and gone ...
Without the joy of angel song;
The hope, which on that blessed night
The shepherds heard in angel light,

Seems all but gone in this our world,
As through long centuries we've been hurled
So far from that celestial night,
When angels sang and stars shone bright.

The Light of Lights at last had come ...
Sin's pain and death to be undone;
By that One Life, lived free of sin
And death, which could not conquer Him!

Yet as we wait, our hope grows dim ...
The promise of new life seems thin;
As weary years have come and gone
And stilled the happy angel song.

Oh God! Remind us once again ...
Our hearts rekindle, stir within;
The fire's flame, the promised Joy
That came to earth ... THE Baby Boy!

"For the revelation awaits an appointed time; it speaks
of the end and will not prove false. Though it linger, wait for it;
it will certainly come and will not delay." Habakkuk 3:2 (NIV)

About the Author

A sojourner who has moved more than 25 times since her marriage, the author understands life as Pilgrimage. Since her early days in the majestic Pacific Northwest, the beauty of nature, music, poetry and Scripture have informed her pursuit of the Transcendent. It is her prayer you will be encouraged and refreshed as you ponder these weekly readings through the year, knowing you are never abandoned on your journey.

CPSIA information can be obtained
at www.ICGtesting.com
Printed in the USA
BVHW031420291118
534322BV00007B/43/P

9 781973 644934